james blunt

back to bedlam

www.jamesblunt.com

© 2005 by International Music Publications Ltd
First published in 2005 by International Music Publications Ltd
International Music Publications Ltd is a Faber Music company
3 Queen Square, London WC1N 3AU

Cover by Salvador Design
Artwork & Design by Bose Collins Ltd & James Blunt
Illustration by Matt Durston
Photography by Steve Double, Lynn Campbell & Cyndi Sayre

Arranging and engraving: Artemis Music Ltd (www.artemismusic.com)
Printed in England by Caligraving Ltd
All rights reserved

ISBN 0-571-52451-6

To buy Faber Music publications or to find out about the full range of
titles available, please contact your local music retailer or Faber Music sales enquiries:
Faber Music Ltd, Burnt Mill, Elizabeth Way, Harlow, CM20 2HX England
Tel: +44 (0) 1279 82 89 82   Fax: +44 (0) 1279 82 89 83
sales@fabermusic.com   fabermusic.com

High

Words and Music by James Blunt and Ricky Ross

run-ning wild____ a - mong____ all the stars____ a - bove. Some - times,____

it's____ hard____ to be - lieve____ you re - mem - ber me.____

- ber____ me.____

You're Beautiful

Words and Music by James Blunt, Sacha Scarbek and Amanda Ghost

♩ = 83

Guitar: Capo 8th fret

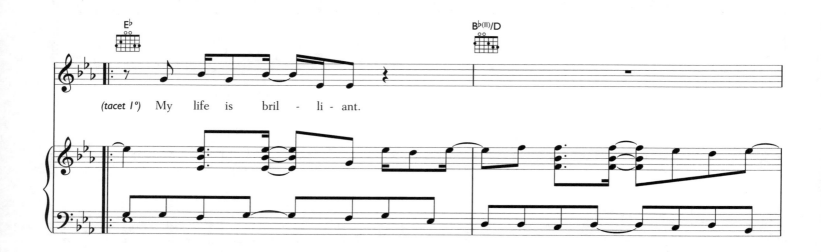

(tacet 1°) My life is bril - li - ant.

Wisemen

Words and Music by James Blunt, Jimmy Hogarth and Sacha Scarbek

Got to ask your-self the ques-tion, where are_ you now?_ where are_ you now?_

Goodbye My Lover

Words and Music by James Blunt and Sacha Scarbek

Tears And Rain

Words and Music by Guy Chambers and James Blunt

1. How I wish I could surrender my soul;
2. How I wish I could walk through the doors of my mind;

shed the clothes that become my skin,
hold memory close at hand,

Out Of My Mind

Words and Music by James Blunt

So Long, Jimmy

Words and Music by James Blunt and Jimmy Hogarth

1. I just can't be - lieve_____ that it's ov - er._____
2. I'm just so re - lieved_____ that it's ov - er._____

glad for the__ ex - per - i - ence,__ we miss you now you've gone.__ We're just

swim - ming in your soul 'cause we all wish we wrote this song. Life__ goes__ on.__

Repeat with organ solo ad lib. to fade

on.__

Billy

Words and Music by James Blunt, Sacha Scarbek and Amanda Ghost

1. Bil-ly's leav-ing to-day, (don't know where he's go-ing). Holds his head in dis-grace,

2. Bil-ly's leav-ing to-day, (don't know where he's go-ing). He's got lines on his face,

Cry

Words and Music by James Blunt and Sacha Scarbek

1. I have seen peace.

(1.) I have seen pain, resting on the shoulders of your name.

(2.) birth. I have seen death. Lived to see a lover's final breath.

And if you want__ to_____ talk__ a - bout__ what will be,__

come and sit with me,__ and cry__

_____ on my shoul - der. I'm__ a friend.__

_____ And if you want__ to_____

No Bravery

Words and Music by James Blunt and Sacha Scarbek